Cardboard
in the sole of my Shoe

The story of a boy growing up in Ferguslie Park

Pat Kidd

Edited by Lisa Nicoll

Copyright @ Pat Kidd 2022

DEDICATION

Betty Kidd
Born 26 December 1934
Died April 6th 2020.

This is our story mum.
The love you had for your children
and the hard work you did
to keep food on the table
and clothes on our backs.

Darkwood Crew
Helping Ferguslie Flourish

Tannahill Centre

ONE
REN

ACKNOWLEDGEMENTS

I would like to say a special thanks to Terry McTernan for the help he has given me along the way while developing the book with Lisa Nicoll and a special big thanks to my wife and best pal, Arlene, for putting up with me for the past two year in writing this book.

Thanks go to the people who sponsored the launch of this book in Ferguslie Park on the 9th of December 2022:

Own Your Bike (SCIO)
Kenneth Keegan Undertakers
NISA aka Mamies
and Morrisons

ABOUT THE AUTHOR

Patrick Kidd was born on the 17th March 1959 to his mum Betty and dad Joe.

His mam came from Ferguslie Park and his dad came from Shortroods. They married and spent most of their married life in Ferguslie Park. They had Joe and then came Pat.

Pat has lived all of his life in Ferguslie Park He works as a taxi driver and lives with his partner Arlene. Pat has been writing short stories for years. This is his first selection of tales that have been edited and published and they chronicle an account of him growing up.

At a young age Pat was told that he was dyslexic and was sent to speech therapy and to a spelling teacher. Pat said, *"In those days the doctors didn't recognize dyslexia and the priest called me disabled."*

Pat has worked with playwright Lisa Nicoll to bring these stories together and to allow the stories to connect with a wider audience.

Ferguslie Park is an urban community situated in the Northwest Paisley area of Renfrewshire. It has a population of 4100 people.

The community has been in a constant state of regeneration since 1969 and has a high level of social capital and community activism.

CHAPTER 1

My earliest memory of my childhood is me in a pram and Joe my brother, with a bit of toast, going round to my granny's house.

I'm in a pram because I've an accident getting a crossbar ride on a big boys bike.

Joe crashed and we came off.

One of the spokes on the wheels broke off and went in one side my leg and out the other.

I had to go into hospital to get it cut out and have an operation.

I can't walk and we don't have a wheelchair, so we've got a pram and a push chair to get me about.

Poor Joe has to take me out to play and push me about.

My Granny watches me, and Joe goes to school.

I'm in the close this one day and I hear my gran moaning to my mam,

"Your away to do two jobs again the day and he never came hame on Friday with the wages again."

My mam says, "He did come hame. He was just late again."

Ma gran laffs at my mam.

"Leave my mam a fucking lone," I shout.

The two of them are shocked.

Ma granny says, "I know where he herd that from."

I tell my mam, "See when am big, am going to get a job and give you my wages on a Friday. I'll come home with my pay pack for you."

My mam cuddles me and sits down on my granny's stairs. She says, "We might need that." And she rubs my head, "I am going to go away and leave you for a while."

I get upset. "No no don't leave me. Sorry I said a bad word to my gran."

My mam smiles, "No it's not that. Am going away and when I come back I will have a surprise for you."

"I don't want a surprise. I want you."

But ma mam goes away and I stay with my gran.

I cry at night.

My aunt comes and takes me out in the pram. She takes me into the shop and gets me a penny tray. After a few days we walk round to my house.

"Is my mam home?" I ask.

The door opens.

Ma dad carrys me into the living room.

My mam is crying. She cuddles me, "I have that surprise I promised you."

And my dad shows me a wee baby.

"I just want you not to leave me again mam."

"I promise," she says.

Then I tell her, "You can take the baby back now."

CHAPTER 2

My stooky's off now.

My scars are healing on my leg, so I learn to walk again.

Ma mams got rid of the push chair that a nabour gave me because I couldn't walk.

I'm back walking and even getting back out to play.

I still go to my grans in the mornings for her to watch.

Yesterday my gran and my aunt took me up the toon and got me school clothes and a new pair of shoes.

My gran moans all the way up the west end.

She must get up out her bed and say to herself "Who can I moan at today!"

My Aunt Teresa rubs me on the head when old moana goes into a shop. "Just walk beside her and walk nice and she will be ok," she says. She gies me a bit of chocolate and tells me, "Eat it before your gran comes out the shop."

Then I hear my Grans voice, "Here you let me see your face. Look at you! Look at him Teresa, he is all chocolate. Did you gie him that? I'm trying to keep him clean to go into shops for a new uniform."

Ma gran spits in her hanky and washes my face. It smells horrible.

"I hope your teeth weren't in that hanky gran," I say.

My aunt Teresa bursts out laffing.

"Do you think that's funny?" ma gran asks.

She tells me I have to be good and if I am when we meet ma mam, we'll go into Storie Street chippy.

I say I'll be good, but when we get to the high street across from the museum ma gran goes into a shop and I notice the shop has a sliding iron gate.

Me and my aunt Teresa walk on a bit to meet my mam at the corner where my mam gives me a cuddle and says, "I hope you've been good for your gran. Where is she?"

Before I can answer we hear my grans voice shouting and my aunt is laffing, "You didney Pat?!"

"I pulled the sliding iron gate over and the padlock was still on it so I locked it."

"Wi your gran inside?" ma mam asks.

"The man in the shops letting her out," I say.

Ma gran see's the funny side of it. "You're some boy," she says. "You're some boy."

CHAPTER 3

My mums famley moved to Paisley. They moved into a tenement in the high street. It was too small, but they all shared and got on with life.

I have no knowledge of my mum's dad.

I think the girls left school and all worked and the men worked from a young age. My Uncle Wully worked in the coal, so the house was always warm. He was a lovable rogue.

My mum says to me I am just like him.

I say, "So, he is to blame!"

My mam laffs.

My uncle made sure though they never went short. One Christmas I was in my grans in Drums Avenue. My gran and my mam were preparing Christmas dinner.

"Where is that Wully Byron," my gran says.

"He will be here mam. He is getting the Turkey for the dinner."

Then the door opens and there he is.

"Where is the Turkey?"

"Here it is," he says.

And I hear the screams from the kitchen.

I go in the lobbie to see what's wrong, and a big Turkey is running about! I shit myself and run.

But someone kills it and dinner is saved.

CHAPTER 4

Its Saturday.

I hear someone in my room, I look, it's my mum.

"Hi Mam," I say in a sleepy voice, wanting to pull the covers back over my head, but I know. I know my mam wants me, so I fling the candlewick off me and get up.

"Do you want to come with me?" she asks.

I don't ask where, I just say ok, and I get ready. We sneak out passed her room and I see ma dad still in bed and I smell the smell of drink coming out the room. We cut through Douglas Street swing park, and I run on to get a shot on the swings before she catches up.

"Come on I'll get you breakfast in Well Street"

We go up Well Street and I look up the street full of shops on either side of the road. You don't have to go up to the west end and into toon to get what you need - everything you need is here – butcher, bakers, dairy, hairdressers.

We go into the butchers where mam has a Christmas club. She gets her butcher meat, and she asks the man to take it off her club money.

Next into Lipton's dairy, the man here has an overall like a coat. He gets my mam's butter off a big block and hits it with two bits of wood to make it square then wraps it in paper.

Back down Well Street again we go, and my mam stops and talks to a man in the street. He's loading a wee white van. I know the man (he is known to everyone in Ferguslie) - it's Mr Hampson the baker.

He gets a bag and fills it with broken fruit cakes, I love fruit cake.

My mam then goes into Bernard's the hairdresser to get her hair done for tonight - my mam has a wedding the day, her and ma dad. She puts me into the Boston café next door and I get my roll and sausage and my tea then I go to the swing park again. The sun is roasting as I wait for my mam. When she comes along, I don't recognise her, her hair is all done it up, in a big *beehive* they call it.

"Feel it Pat," she says.

It's solid.

"You look nice mam."

It's great to see my mam nice, it's always us she works for.

She smiles at me, and we head back down the road.

CHAPTER 5

My aunts and gran and ma mam are getting my brother Joe new school clothes.

Ma mam tells me, "Joseph is making his first holy communion."

Holy communion is a special day in a boys and girls life in St Fergus's School in Ferguslie Park.

"When your in school you will do the same."

"I hope I don't mam. I hate new clothes."

Then I hear my mams sister, my aunt Mary going, "Betty it the provedent woman at the door."

Provedent woman is where my ma gets a wee book of tickets and that buys us our clothes. We then pay the women weekly. But if ma dad dosen't come home with his wages on a Friday, and she chaps the door, we get told to hide behind the chairs cause we have no money to pay her.

This week though she has gave my mam a provedent check cause after Joe's communion there's gonna be a wee party in the community centre in Blackstone Road.

Everyone will make sandwiches and Mr Hampson is gonna get us cakes, pies sausage rolls.

My Granny Kidd turns up at the house. I like my granny. She comes from Shortroods. She is very small she has worked in Makettes chip shop for years.

She is known as wee Anne. She has a wee coat and wee boots on.

I run and give her a hug.

She has a bag. I open it and there is clothes for me and a toy.

"There for you to look good in on Saturday," she tells me.

Saturday. Joe's big day has come.

Ma mam is so proud.

Then I hear my dad saying, "Pat come here."

On the bed is the clothes my gran got me. Ma dad puts them on me. A wee brown suit with short trousers and a wee white shirt.

I am walking up Westburn Avenue to Blackstone Road to St Fergus's.

My dads gets a hold of me and Joe's walking wi my mam.

"Make sure he stays clean," she shouts tay ma dad.

We get in the chapel. Everyone is saying how smart I am. Me and ma dad sit on a bench during the service. My dad goes to see my mam. He comes back and he cant find me. I am in a wee room at the side.

I hear them looking for me.

Then my gran grabs me. "Whit are you doing in there Pat!"

"A pee, am busting."

My gran drags me out of the wee room, "That's the confession box!!" Then she drags me off to the toilet.

CHAPTER 6

"You are nothing Kidd. Nothing. Do you hear me?"

I look up and I see him coming towards me.

Franky is sitting next to me, "Fuck Pat we're in bother."

I say, "How are we in bother?"

Then this priest is at my desk, "Are you listening to me?!" and he goes to slap me with his big hand.

I get out the way and go to run out the class. I nearly knock Franky over.

The priest shouts, "Come here you two."

I say, "Franky never done anything it was me."

The priest throws a blackboard duster at me.

Franky shouts, "Missed."

And we run out the class.

We go to run out the front door of the school.

Sister Ella calls after us, "Paddy come here."

Sister Ella is always nice to me. She knows I have problems reading and my spelling is a disaster but she knows there is something wrong.

Sister Ella tells Franky to take me in the Gym Hall and hide and then says, "I'm going to talk to father Pat, he has a horrible attitude to you, he doesn't like you."

Franky tells Sister Ella, "That old basterd doesn't like himself!"

We pass the tuck shop and its open and no ones there.

We take a couple of golden cups and then hide in the gym.

Sister Ella keeps her promise and comes and finds us, she tells us, "He doesn't want youse two in the school never mind his class. But the headmaster has given me permission to teach you."

To sister I say, "Where do you get all those fancy words from?"

Franky bursts out laffing and so does sister Ella, "Whit am I going to do with you!?" she laughs.

And Franky says, "Get us a golden cup."

Me and Franky start to hang about after school.

And Sister Ella, Franky and me become good pals.

CHAPTER 7

It's a Sunday morning. My clothes are ready. My mam has ironed them and put them out in the living room.

Joe has his own clothes ready. He is going out with his pal George.

"Pat Pat come here." My mam gives me a note to go to the shops in falcon crescent.

"You'd think I was a wane given me a note. I run about there way my pals."

I get a clip in the head, "That's for been smart," she says.

"Ok ok mam point taken."

I shout in Sheba my German shepherd dog.

We are so close.

She follows me everywhere.

We get into the shops.

The Roberert - the name of the shop we get sausage, eggs, bacon and plain breed.

Sheba barks. She wants to carry the sausages

I tell her she's no getting them.

The man gives me a pack of tights called American tan and something he puts in a brown bag. He puts them in a carrier bag.

The dog is still barking to get something to carry. I give her the brown bag.

She runs on in front throwing it up in the air.

I give her a row.

We get to the close.

My mums nabour picks up the bag. It is ripped and there are things hanging out of it with two bits of string that's stuck on each end.

My mams looking out the window.

I shout up to her, "The dogs ripped up your women things."

"Get up here. You and your dog. Why did you give the dog them to carry?"

"I should have given her the sausage to carry," I say.

She is looking at my dad and he is laffing.

"What you laffing at," I ask.

I no what your mam is going to say.

Before I can open ma mouth she says, "How did you no gie the dog the fking papers to carry. You were to get the Sunday papers. Ooo but your no a wane and you don't need a note. Go back and get the papers. We're going to chapel at 12. Your some boy."

CHAPTER 8

We're called to a room where there's a nurse.

She's looking at everyone's heed and putting this purple stuff on them.

It stinks and we're told we aren't allowed to wash it off till we get home.

The head teacher then comes in and tells us, "It's important to wash yir head."

I stand up, "Well we'll need to wash our heeds now with all this purple shit on them."

"Go to my office," he shouts.

He gives me a note to give to my mam.

My mam finds the note and she goes up and sees him and has words with him. "Nits don't come from a dirty head you know."

My hair gets washed and my mam gets this wee metal comb she pulses through my hair and it cracks the wee things on my head on her nail. But when am in my bed I can still smell that purple stuff on my head.

CHAPTER 9

Ever since we were wanes, ma mam has had two jobs to put food in our bellys.

She gets up early and takes me and Joe in a pram to my grans in Drums Avenue.

My gran moved her famley from Ireland where she worked as a chapel cleaner. Don't know why the candles didnae blow out when the old basterd went near them. Her face could put them out.

She doesn't like me and I don't like her. She has her favourites.

My mam comes from a close famley, two brothers and her four sisters.

My grans house is always full when I am growing up, especially on a Saturday but I don't like going.

Gran dies and everybody is in her house.

All of us wanes are in the bedroom. Some off us are lying on the bed with all the coats covering us up. I love it.

Then I have a thought and I go through all the pockets and get all the coins.

I hear all the adults singing. I sneak up to the living room door and look in. My aunts and uncles are all drinking around this big, long box. It's open.

Then the door opens.

My mam comes out in the room and says, "Get to sleep."

"Am waiting on you mam. Am no staying with ma granny she always moans."

Joe takes me away in the kitchen, "Listen give my mam peace," he says.

"Am no staying. I don't like my old gran."

Joe says, "Stop that Pat. She is dead."

I don't feel sad. I ask where she is and Joe tells me she is in the living room in the big box.

"That's the lid", he says point at a lid lying against the kitchen wall.

"We need to put the lid on the box in case she gets out," I say.

Joe just laffs, "Don't say that to my mam."

The next day I am in school. The nuns takes my class across to the chapel. We are all singing. I think it's the sky boat song.

I say to my teacher, "One of those boxes was in my grans house last night."

"That's the box that was in your grans. This is her funeral."

"Whit does that mean?"

"I will tell you later."

I don't know why but I feel sad when we are singing the sky boat song.

CHAPTER 10

There's a new boy that's starting to hang about wi me and Franky. His name is Mik. When we get out of school we say we'll met him at the keep left and we'll hang around his bit. We meet him at his bit at the Admiral Oval.

A say to him, "Is this the undesirables around here? Here and Holborn Avenue?"

"Aye it is." Mik says.

He takes us to the brandy burn. Then he goes into a shop called minzees. He comes out the shop and shouts, "Run!"

So we do.

Into his street.

The guy chasing us doesn't come into Mik's street.

Me and Franky ask, "Whit happened?"

Mik geez us sweets. We laf.

"This place is ok." Franky says. "We're moving in!"

When I get hame that night I say to my mam, "Can we get a house in the undesirables?"

She looks at me, "No we cannot."

Come Saturday we meet Mik again.

"Where are we going?" I ask.

"Come on," he says.

We follow him and head to the racecourse playing fields.

Mik says, "We'll go to the airport to steal a plane."

"That sounds good to me," I say.

We go into the airport grounds. We see a fountain coming. Mik jumps in strait away. It's got money in it. It's a fucking luck fountain. Am in straight away alang wi Franky. We all grab money and fill our pockets.

We hear a voice, "Come here youse!"

And we run like hell over the racecourse. The coins are waying us down, but we get away.

CHAPTER 11

Its Sunday night and on Friday when I came in from school, I planked my shoes under my bed.

"Pat Pat come here this minute."

I walk into the room. I see my mam sitting on the bed holding ma shoes the soles facing up the way with a big hole in one of the shoes. She takes them into ma dad.

He cleans the shoes.

"Why did you plank your shoes?" My mam asks.

"Is it because one has a hole in the sole?

When did you dae that?"

"It wisney me," I say

"Who was it then?" my dad says.

"Well you no we have big mice in the house."

On the way back from ma granny's last Saturday my mam stole a loan of the chapel cat to catch the mice. So, it must have been the mice that eat a hole in my shoe."

My Dad shouts on ma mam, "Betty Betty come here. Tell your mam what you just told me."

"I heard him," she says, "Now get out ma site."

We get a bath for school on a Sunday night. I am the last one in the bath because I got seen peeing in it when I was first in. Now when I get to go in the bath the water is that freezing, I want out.

Ma dad says to stay in. He comes in with pots of hot water.

When we get up in the morning, I get ready. My mam has cut a bit of lino and a bit of cardboard and put them in my shoe where the hole is. My mam tells me to wear them while she gets me a new pair. She waits for the shop to open then she comes to my school, and I put my new shoes on.

CHAPTER 12

I hear a loud mouth voice coming into my classroom.
I say to Franky, "Who the fk is this?"
He catches me talking to Franky, "You boy come here."
I know he is talking to me but ma dad told me to ignore bullies, so I do.
He throws a black board duster at me and it just misses.
My pal calls out, "Missed."
I bust out laffing and say, "Your lucky that didnae hit me."
"Get out get out. You will never learn anything. Your nothing. You will be nothing. Go to the office and wait for me. I have a class to teach."
I am sitting outside the office.
He comes along the corridor. He sees me sitting on the chairs. He goes daft, "Get in here."
He is sitting behind his desk with his hand on a bit of wood on the desk - Father Canning it says.
"You will not be allowed in my classrooms till I speak to your dad. Get out of this school."
He picks up a metal ruler and slams it down on my finger.
It cuts the tap bit nearly off.

I cry. But I remember what my dad said about bullies - pick something up and hit them with it.

So, I do.

I pick the ruler up and hit him in the face with it.

I stop crying and run out the room.

When I get home my mam looks at my finger and takes me to hospital. I get stitches.

She asks, "What happened?"

So I tell her.

"When you go to school tomorrow I will come out the cleaners office and I will see this man. A headmaster doing that."

"But I hit him too mam and it wasent the headmaster it was the priest."

She nearly chokes, "The priest? The priest?"

So I get the rest of the week off.

My mam takes me to my granny Kidd and I know I will be ok. My granny loves me and she sticks up for me. Ma granny says I remind her of my grandad. My dad is staying there as my mam threw him out for drinking too mutch.

We chap the door. When my gran opens it she is pleased to see us.

My mam asks if ma dad is in.

Ma granny says he is at work but will be home soon.

Gran makes a pot of tea. The teapot had a woolly hat on it - a tea cosy they call it. They sit at a table looking out the window.

"What happened to the boys hand?" my grandad says.

My mam tells him.

He goes into another room and comes and gives me some coins.

My grandad tells ma mam, ma dads no been drinking.

My dad comes in.

He grabs me and cuddles me.

I cry, "He's hurt my hand."

My dad asks me, "Why did you hit the priest?"

"You told me if a bully hits you hit him back with something if he's bigger than you, so I did."

The next day me and my dad are in the headmasters office.

The headmaster starts to talk to my dad.

My dad says,"I want to talk to him. The priest."

"The priest," I say in a lower voice.

The priest comes into the room.

My dad says, "Talk to me."

"Your boy hit me with a ruler in the face. That's why he is barred from school."

I say, "You hit me with the ruler and cut the top off my finger and I got stitches."

"Why did you hit my boy?"

"I was trying to learn him Latin."

"Whits Latin?

He goes to speech therapist cause he can hardly speak English.

"Don't hit my boy or anyone belonging to me."

I am so proud of my dad.

I walk out the school with him and the headmaster calls my name, "Pat Pat this is your new teacher, Sister Ella."

CHAPTER 13

Father Canning calls me into his office. He tells me he doesn't want me or ma pal Franky in St Fergus's again. Not while he is still there.

"He is trying to get me to let you go to a special school Pat," ma mam says,

What am I going to do? I will just run away. This is the last thing my mam has to worry about. I look over and my mam is crying.

"Mam, mam, I won't do that."

I cuddle her and my brother rubs the top of my head.

I go in the room. I don't want my mam to see me cry. Then I shout out, "No no. You have to talk to Sister Ella."

"Whits sister Ella has got to do with anything?" mam asks.

I tell ma mam that she heard the priest was hitting me and trying to hit Franky. She had words with the heady and she is going to be wur teacher. We like her.

"I will talk to her tomorrow," mam says.

I go round to get Franky to go to school.

"Do you want to hide down the farm?" Franky says.

"No, we're to meet my mam and Sister Ella."

We go in through the big doors and the headmaster's office is in front of us. My mam puts us in the cleaner's office. She works as a cleaner in the school.

Mr Ogg the janitor takes us in because Father Canning sees us and is coming towards us.

Ma mam and Sister Ella stop him.

Mr Ogg tells ma mam, Sister Ella and Father Canning to go into his office.

The door closes.

CHAPTER 14

Sister Ella has taken to me in school. She has asked me to stay behind. She knows that's no the kind a thing ah da but something happened that day that I did stay behind.

She says, "Thanks Paddy."

I never got called Paddy before and never again by anyone else other than Sister Ella. She knew I struggled.

I sat on the flair and so did she.

She spoke to me about my mum doing two jobs. About my dad going away on the drink and keeping his wages.

I put my head down so she never new I was sad and nearly crying.

But I was wrong she knew all along.

I wasn't upset about my dad drinking and my mam doing two jobs. Loads of women in feegie do two jobs. It was just that for the first time someone seen my problem and cared. She is a holy person but she knows what to do with me. She hits me on tap on the head with the ruler.

"Can you do something for me and you starting tomorrow?"

"Aye I will," I says.

She taps me on the head again.

I say to her, "Do you think you're Father Canning?"

We laff, "Can you do the milk for me? I will call you the milk monitor."

I laff and say, "Better that than been called thick by that basterd Father Canning."

Just then the door opens.

It's ma mam, "Has he been kept back sister? Am sorry."

Sister Ella smiles, "No no he hasn't. I have a new best friend."

My mam rubs my head, "That's the first good report about you I have had. Well done."

CHAPTER 15

I get home from school one night just a couple of weeks before the school holidays and ma dad sits me down on the massive couch, I look so small on.

He says, "If you're good at school the next two weeks I'll come home from work without going to the pub and on the Friday, you finish up school you can go out and play every day."

My mind is thinking about being on holiday fae school and going down to cowboy valley where the old wooden prefab houses used to be to play cowboys and Indians with ma pals.

I'm thinking about going down the racecourse and seeing the big shows - the dive bommers where the one at the top is nearly in the clouds. And the waltzers! I love the waltzers.

And I say, "Deal."

Then my ma says to my dad, "Tell him, tell him whit I say."

And my Da looks at me and says, "Promise, if you're good we've booked a week in Butlins."

"Where's that?" I ask.

"In Ayr," am told.

An I say, "Ayr's about a day away! I'll be good. I promise."

I go to my bed and as am heading down the lobby I hear my da say to my Mam.

"Do you think he will do it?"

And my Mam says, "He'll try."

CHAPTER 16

My man is having a word with ma da. I hear her and ma dad in the living room as I walk up the lobbie.

'I am getting pulled in by Father Canning for our Pat no going to chapel on a Sunday," she says.

"Can you talk to him. Just talk to him."

Ma dad opens the living room door. I am standing at the outher side of the door on the lobbie.

"Come here Pat," Dad says. "You need to go to chapel. You hear me?"

I says, "Da am not doing my chores in the house for me to put my shilling in the plate in the chapel. Its no fair. I'll go to chapel if you want me to. But you no what I'll do. I'll put my shilling in and take two out."

And that's me in trouble again.

"Ok," he says.

"You will work on a Sunday in the house. On a Sunday you can wash the lino around the carpet."

Our carpet never went right up to the skirting board.

It went about 2 feet short and the lino went the rest of the way to the skirting. So I had to wash the lino on a Sunday instead of going to chapel.

CHAPTER 17

We're on the bus going to secondary school - St Aelreds in Glenburn. It's a few miles from Ferguslie. We get a free bus to take us there. On the bus Mike is up the back smoking wi other boys. They have long hair. That's the style.

So I decide I am going to grow mine.

"Here take a draw of that fag," Mike says.

I shake my head, "No its ok."

"Take a draw," he says again.

I take one.

I think am going to pass out.

A voice says to me, "Don't smoke if you don't like it Pat."

It was the guy down the stairs fae me. He is older than me. I have always wanted to talk to him.

"Don't copy him to look tough." But this guy is smoking and he says, "Your looking at me because am saying don't smoke. But I have been smoking for a long time. Well it feels like that."

We get talking. He is called Gordon. But he says to call him Halfpint. He says my big brother Joe called him that and it's stuck.

We get to school he says, "I will get you at dinner time."

I am looking forward to dinner time. I feel older. I have a new mate.

Dinner time comes.

"Am going to the canteen," I say.

"Come on," Halfpint says.

I follow him and we go to the Braehead shops.

"Whit you getting?" he says.

"Ah don't know," I say.

He gets a roll pie and brown sauce so I get it too.

"Its brilliant."

"Stick way me pal."

He has given me a new name. I am Kiddy now after my name Kidd.

In the afternoon in class we're in the upstairs class Mike Bryce and Tam are smoking.

Someone shouts, "Here's Mr Quinn."

Panic.

I have a desk. We lift the lid up and put the fags in there.

The teacher is writing on the black board.

Franky says, "Your desk. Your desk is on fire."

There were papers in the desk where we put the fags. All you see is smoke. Teacher goes daft and throws me out the door of the class.

I fall on the stairs.

"Stand there boy," he says.

I do but when he comes out he throws me against the wall.

I say, "It wasnt me. I don't smoke."

He slaps my face.

I get the strap aff Mr Madden the headmaster.

CHAPTER 18

My Granny Kidd has come to our house from Shortroods - a skeem next to the airport. That's where my dad came from before he married my mum. She has come to collect me as I have not been good at school.

My dad's not come home.

It's Friday. Wages nights.

She has come to help my mam, "You'd better behave for your gran," my mam tells me.

My gran says, "Am telling you he will. He is good with me and his grandad."

We go to the chip shop cause grandad wants a fish supper. Then we get home tae my grans home.

I hear a voice coming out the toilet, "Is that the torag Annie?"

My grandad comes out the toilet with shaving foam on his face and a vest, "You ok son?" he asks me.

"Yes grandad."

He is a spotless man that always works. My gran irons his shirt and his coller. He is staying in but always gets dressed.

"There is my pay on the fireplace Annie and give the boy the horse."

It's a wee solid leather horse. He always gives me it.

"You can get that when your older as long as you don't turn out like your father."

"He is only a boy," my gran says.

"He has got to know that after you finish work on a Friday come home with your pay and don't go away and get drunk like him."

"Ok grandad."

We sit at the big coal fire. Grandad gets a big fork and puts bread on the end of it. He puts it up against the fire and makes us toast. My gran gies us a cup of tea.

I hear the door. My gran gets it. It is my dad. She takes him in the bedroom. He is drunk. My grandad gets up and goes in the bedroom.

"Stay there pal," he tells me.

I hear my grandad shouting at my dad. "You drink and then get all sad and come here to look for sympathy aff your mam. Your wife and wanes feel feart in case you don't come home on a Friday. Don't drink. Go home to your wife and wanes. Think of your wanes. That's why Pat's here. He has got into trouble at school again".

Then my grandad says something I don't understand, "The wrong ones died. Your brother and sister died. You live and look at the way youve turned out."

I hear my da crying. I feel sad and sorry for my dad. I haven't seen my dad cry before.

My gran comes back into the living room.

I ask her, "Is my dads brother and sister dead?"

"Your dad will tell you," she says.

I go to my bed.

My granny always makes sure my bed's warm.

A big candlewick she calls it.

I hear my dad come in. He sits on the bed.

"Dad," I say. "What was my grandad talking about when he said the wrong ones died?"

My dad's head goes down.

I kneel up on the bed and put my arms around his neck. "Don't cry dad am sad when I see you cry."

"Listen son when I was your age I had a brother and a sister."

"When can I see them dad?" I ask.

"You can't son. They took ill. Not well. They were taken into hospital. They never came out."

"How no dad?"

"They died son."

I wouldn't like it if my brother Joe died, I would cry all the time. Me and my dad lay on the bed, and I cry myself to sleep in my dads arms.

CHAPTER 19

The next day my gran makes me boiled egg. She cuts my toast into soldiers. Then I hear my gran in the room.

She says to my dad, "Your dads working half day then he's takin Pat to the football. So, you get up. This room is stinking of stale drink and its coming from you. It's no fair on that wane. That wane that's supposed to be your son, sleeping next to you smelling like that. Your a disgrace. That wee lassie you married works two jobs to put food in your wanes mouth so you can disappear with your pay packet. Get hame and sort yourself out before you don't have a famley."

"Are we going to win today grandad?"
"Ma boy it's East Fife we are playing. And if your good we will get a program." My grandad is trying to make me feel safe because I heard whit, he said to my dad about him being dead like his brother and sister.

But he doesn't need to. I know my grandad loves me and my granny. We leave to go to the football.

When we get there my grandad gives me a lifty over - that means I get in for nothing!

A man comes round the ground with boxes of macaroon bars. I get a macaroon bar.

St Mirren win 3 /1. All the men wave there bonnets in the air. We walk up to Moss Street to get The Times and The Citizen - two Scottish sports papers that come out on a Saturday night after the football. The men check their football results in the papers one.

When we get back to my grans there is a lovely smell of cooking.

"Do I smell homemade soup for me and the boy, Annie," my grandad asks.

"You do that. And totties, cabbage and ham wa real butter. Only the best for my boys."

"Thanks gran, I love you."

CHAPTER 20

I go home on the Sunday. My grandad gives me ten bob. "Don't let your father see that. He will take it aff you. Get yourself something nice with it."

It's a warm Sunday. We have dinner and my mam sends me to the ice cream van with a bowl and he fills it up. I love Jackaneles ice cream.

My mam opens a tin of peaches. We have ice cream and peaches.

Then my dad says, "We will go a walk down the farm."

I say to my brother Joe, "Whit the fuck is up with him?"

"He came home with my gran," Joe says. "He is on his last legs. Fuck the two he had on Friday night were no good to him"

I tell Joe, "They didn't keep him up when he came to my granny's door. Grandad went mad at him and stuck up for my mam."

"I know gran came around wa Dad when you were at the football and gave mam money in an envelope and said she had to take it and that she didn't deserve whit he does to her and the wanes. Says he isn't going to the Greenhill for drink today."

"That's a first," I say.

My mam hears me. She hits me on the head and says, "Give him a chance, ok? For your mam."

We are down the farm clapping the horses and cows. My mam has plastic bags that have wee bottles of ginger for us. I take them. I climb through the fence and head for a field. I start to pull leaves out the ground.

"Whit are you doing?" Joe asks.

"Watch," I say. I bend down and pull up totties. Then I fill the bags and run back to my mam and dad.

My dad asks, "Whit have you got there?"

He looks and says, "Pat, I thought you were going to change?"

"I have! It was Joseph!"

My Dad calls my brother Joseph not Joe.

My mams bust out laffing at me. "Let's go hame and I'll make chips for pieces and chips."

CHAPTER 21

My wee cousins David and Eric are staying with us just now. Their we brother Allan is in the sick children's hospital. He is very ill. He has leukaemia.

His mum, my mum's sister Brenda, brought them down to my mums to stay.

Wee Eric and David are sleeping in my room.

There are two single beds - one against each wall.

My German shepherd Sheba sleeps on the floor beside my bed.

That night I am out with my pals down at Falcon Crescent shops. Its getting dark. We head home - me Halfpint and Romeo. Halfpint stops for a pee in a shop doorway. The doorway is dark and we hear Halfpint arguing with a man and woman in the doorway.

The man starts to attack our Halfpint. Me and Romeo run back to help our pal. The man is hitting Halfpint and we get into a fight. We leave the man sitting on the ground wi the woman

"I know youse," the woman shouts.

We go home. I don't tell ma mam.

I get my tea and toast and go to bed where my wee cousins are. My wee cousins like staying with my mam. Joe is sleeping in the living room on the bed setee.

I am shitting myself in case the women did know us.

Every time I hear the close door open I think it is the police. Then my worst nightmare comes true. The close door opens. I hear Halfpint's door getting chapped. Its a police chap. I can hear them asking for Gordon. Then I hear them go into his house.

I hear his mam saying to the police, "Don't forget his pal up the stair Pat."

Then my door goes. My mam opens it. It's the police. "Is Pat in?"

"What for?" my mam asks.

"There was an assault in Falcon Crescent. Pat and Gordon were involved. We have a witness," the police say.

My mam is mad and embarrassed because my wee cousins are staying. "He is in that room," she says.

They come in and go to switch the light on but there is no bulb. One of the police grabs me. But that's a big mistake as they don't see my dog, Sheba.

When the police grab me, she attacks to protect me. The police run out the room.

My mam comes in with the police. She is angry and tells the police to give me a doing. They take me to the police station.

My dad and my brother Joe come to the police station in Mill Street and get me out.

My mam doesn't speak to me for a few days.

CHAPTER 22

Ferguslie Park Avenue is a long avenue full of trees each side of the main road. The buses run up and down these - big doubles decker buses with the door open at the back. Where the bus conductor stands there's a silver pole you grab when you jump on at the back of the bus.

Along the Avenue there's tenements where people stay called veranda blocks. Verandas are where you keep your coal bunkers.

It's the Thursday before the Paisley fair. Ferguslie folk are so happy having a drink out on their verandas.

One day to go before the fair. Me and ma da have kept wer deal. I have been good at school - well no been caught! And he has come home fae work without going to the pub.

My da says, 'You've done well"

And I say, "So have you."

He tells me I have to go and meet my mam from her work tomorrow and take my wee sister. My mam stops for her holidays. Me and my sister are at the Ferguslie Mill gates. There are a lot of people waiting for their mams.

The big massive gates are closed.

When you look through the gates up a long cobbled street there's big buildings to the side – that's where my mam and all the women work.

There's a big siren sound and then out they come, hundreds of women running down the cobbles to get to the gates to get to their boys and girls.

"It's Fair Friday," someone shouts.

All the women cheer.

We go along the west end into the butchers then Liptons Dairy, we're going to Butlins in the morning and Mam's buying food and stuff we need.

We pass the pubs in the west end and I say to my mam, "Do you think ma, da will come home?"

She laughs and we keep walking up the road.

As we pass a pub called the Bubbin, my dad's standing outside. He's standing there waiting on us. He rubs my head.

"Thanks da," I say.

CHAPTER 23

A few weeks later ma dad comes into my granny Kidds living room. It's Friday night and me and my granny sit eating wur supper looking out the window.

Ma dad steals some of my chips. He sits at the table next to me at the window where my gran sits with her friend Mrs Roach.

"Dad why didn't you come home today with your pay and instead you went and got drunk and spent it. Do you hate me, Dad? I heard my grandad say about his kids dying and you living. Do you wish I was dead? Is it me that's making you run away and get drunk? My mam does two jobs and brings her wages in and she doesn't get drunk and run away. If it is me, I will run away."

Then a shout, "Listen to the boy you fking clown. Listen to him before it's too late."

My dad is crying.

So am I.

CHAPTER 24

School holidays.
The world cup is on.
I am allowed out later.
We meet up with the rest of the boys in the street.
We are all playing football every day in the clinic in Westburn. We stand in line and two guys pick their team. Your hoping your no the last one picked. That means you're shit.

Gogs is picking one team and Basil Brian Walsh is picking the other. Basil picks me in his team.

We play away at football all day. We all want a football team we can play with. So someone says we should join the Boys Brigade. So we do and we play for their football team.

We are winning all the games and the priest comes to my door one night. I am in my room listening to my record player. I have started listening to music since hanging around with Halfpint.

My door of my room is open. My mam tells me to come in the living room.

The priest is sitting talking to my mam.

My dad is not talking to him because of what he did to my finger when I was younger.

He tells me to sit down.

"You no whit am here for?" he says.

"No, I don't. Am not in your school now."

"But your in my parish."

"Yir whit?" I ask.

"Your famley go to my chapel and you go to a place called a youth club on a Friday night called the Boys Brigade is that correct?"

"Aye you're right and it's great!"

"Why don't you go to the scouts on a Friday along with your brother Joeseph?" he says. "I want to see you there on Friday night"

I laff because I see my dads head turning around.

"What ar you laffing at boy?" the priest says.

"You telling me what to do. I have been to the scouts they're shit. My pals don't go to it. They go to the Boys Brigade. So ah will be there on Friday night and playing football for them on Saturday with my pals."

"They are a different religion than you. You are not going there."

Then a raised voice from my dad, "I don't preach religion to my boy and tell him who to hang around with. It doesn't matter if his pals go to a different school. If he wants to go to the Boys Brigade he will. Don't you tell him what to do. I am his dad so get out my house."

The priest leaves.

"Thanks Dad."

"You get in your room," he says.

He isn't angry with me though I can tell by his smile.

CHAPTER 25

We go to the Boys Brigade on a Friday night with all the boys in the street. It's the 30th Boys Brigade in Ferguslie Park.

We learn a lot.

As well as playing fitba we do gymnastics and we are good at it.

Halfpint has another reason for going to it - we get out a bit later. After the BB we meet up with outher boys and lassies.

"Your a bad influence on me", I say to him.

"We're ok our ma and dads have a wee drink on a Friday night," he says.

"Ok."

This lassie sits beside me.

"Your in luck," Halfpint says.

But then I hear a voice, "Pat Pat." Its my mam.

Its passed the time I should have been in for.

My mam is in her housecoat standing in the close. "Come on you. Hame."

I would never fall out with my mam. I get up and head out the close. I am worried how the other boys will slag me for my mam coming to get me. I hear Halfpints voice, he says, "Mrs Kidd has my mam sent you to get me to?"

"Aye she has Gordon." My mam never called him Halfpint.

"That was nice what you just done," I say to Halfpint, "said your mam told ma mam to get you too and she didn't."

"I wanted to go hame anyway," he says.

When we get home my dad asks me what we did at the Boys Brigade. I tell him we did gymnastics and that it was great. I tell him we had to run and do a somersault.

In the tenements in Feegie we had a big, long lobbie. My dad being drunk says, "I will show you how to do a summersault. I went to the Boys Brigade when a was a boy. So watch."

"Aye but you wurna steaming drunk when you done your somersaults," ma mam says.

My mam and me look out the window.

There's always a table at the windows in the skeem.

There is always things happening when you look out the window.

"Its Friday mam, I wonder what we will see the night."

Then my mam says, "Here's Mr Glen coming."

Mr Glen always always sings. He yodels. They call him the yodeler.

"Here's his dog come to meet him," I say.

It's a big dog. It didn't have a name but everyone called it *Heyyou*.

I start to tell a story to my mam about the dog, but I don't get my last words out cause we hear a massive bang.

The house shakes.

We run into the lobbie and my dad is laying in a corner. He was trying to do a somersault drunk. It went wrong. We laff and leave him there.

CHAPTER 26

"How the fuck do you build a dooket never mind keep pigeons?" I ask Halfpint.

But Halfpint has come up with this idea ever since my mam came looking for me when I never went straight hame from the Boys Brigade and we were with the lassies – Maggie and big Sandra. We were sitting on the stairs.

Halfpint and Maggie were winching.

Sandra started carrying on with me. She started to lean against me. A hivney had a girlfriend before an was crapping myself. We were just about to kiss and I heard, "Pat your mams coming up the stairs."

The two lassies hid up the stairs.

Me and Halfpint headed down and met my mam.

"Right you two. Hame," she said.

So the pigeon idea sounds good. It takes us a week to build the dooket. All the wood comes from the old tenement next to us.

We get a couple of pigeons. We watch the birds pairing off in the dooket.

"That would have been me and big Sandra if ma mam hadn't came and got us," I say.

Halfpint busts out laffing, "Plenty of time my pal plenty of time."

Later Franky says, "Thursday there is a dance on in the chapel hall. It's called the Feegie flam. Are you going mate."

"I of course I am," I says.

With Halfpint in the dooket I tell him about the Feegie flam.

"We're going," he says.

"That Maggie and big Sandra will be there."

Thursday night.

Am smelling good.

My brother's Karate aftershave on.

Before I go out, him and his girlfriend Irene are kidding me on about Sandra.

At the dance am up dancing. The next song is the last dance, Puppy Love. It's a slow dance.

"Stay up for this one," Sandra says.

Halfway through it, she pulls my head and starts to kiss me. It's a great feeling. I don't want the record to end.

"Are you walking me home?"

"Aye I will."

The four of us are going along the road. Me and Sandra start kissing again. Its brilliant. I haven't done this before.

Its brilliant.

Then I hear Halfpints voice, "Pat come on let's go."

Sandra asks me, "When will I see you?"

"Come round the morrow we will be in the dooket."

She grabs and kisses me again.

Halfpint shouts, "Time to go pal."

CHAPTER 27

It's cold frozen. The ground is white.

I am the first one up and there's nae coal fire on. Am first one up because I am going out delivering the milk.

I hear the voice from outside.

"Pat Pat."

I open the windae. It's Franky waiting on me to go to work. He is like a frozen snotter.

I shout down, "You'll waken ma maw up."

I step out the close and I nearly fall on my arse. It's like a sheet of ice. I have a canvas sack.

Franky says, "Whit's that for?"

"We have na coal. The hoose is freezing. My willie wisnae come out ta dae a pee."

Franky bust out laffing, "Whits the bag for?"

"We're going to knock coal when we deliver the milk," I say. "My mam's got nane till Friday. We just need a couple of bits from a few bunkers that will keep the house warm till then."

We arrive at the depot and the milk float is loaded. Franky grabs the sack and disappears into a big massive fridge. Big clouds of frost comes out as he opens the door. This fridge is bigger than ma house!

I go and look for him. I open the door, everything is white.

"Franky Franky," I shout.

I hear him.

"Whit whit the fuck are you daeing?"

He comes running out. His jumper is like white ice. The sack has got stuff in it. We get on the milk float.

"Franky," I say, "Its warmer out here than in that big fucking fridge!"

We put the stuff Franky stole between the credits of milk. The milk bottles are frozen when you first lift them. We deliver the milk and steal coal from the coal bunkers when we can. Franky divides whit he stole out the big fridge. Big blocks of cheese, butter and bottles of cream.

Now we are talking to lassies though, we need mare money. Franky comes up wi an idea – getting a job on Pinkies farm. The money is better than delivering milk

"Ok," I say.

"We will go tae the farm next week."

"Fae the milk to the farm mate!" Franky says.

"Do you think we could get a Turkey there!"

"We will try mate!"

When I get hame I put the coal in the bunker and fill the fire wi coal for my mam coming in.

Then I fill the fridge and go out and meet my first girlfriend Sandra.

CHAPTER 28

It's a long hot summer the dooket has turned into a great idea. Me and Halfpint have persuaded our maws to let us stay out.. We lite a fire in the back door.

"Where can we put these pigeons till the paint drys?" I say.

I say, "Come with me."

We sneak up the stairs to my landing. Outside my door I've a lockup where my mam keeps everything like her brush and shovel. I open the door and put the pigeons in the lockup till the paint dries.

And we head back to the dooket to sleep. It's about 1 o'clock in the morning. We hear a noise. I am shitting myself as there is a lot of trouble with the older guys in the skeem. We think someone is trying to break in.

"Come on," I say. I open the door.

There's a guy there. He has a big knife.

I look at his hands. They are all blood.

Am wishing I was in my bed.

"You ok wee man," he says to me. "Your Joe's wee brother, aren't you?"

"Aye, Joe's my brother," I say.

"Joe's my pal, a good pal of mine but you havenae seen me ok."

"I haven't seen nobody," I say.

"Your a good boy. Watch yourself."

Then he goes away.

Thank God he is away.

We go in the dooket to go to sleep. The rain is lashing down. Then we're woken up by a woman screaming. It's my mams voice screaming, "Pat I am going to kill you! Come here the two of youse."

We run over to the close. The rain is heavy. We get in the close and there are pigeons flying about.

"Oh no whit happened mam?" I say.

"Happened?! she says. "I am going to my wee cleaning job that I do on a Sunday. I look out the window. It's raining and my brolly is in the lockup. I open it and the pigeons fly out at me."

"Mam we haven't had rain for weeks. I thought it would be ok."

"Get them out this close and in that dooket," she shouts.

While we are putting the pigeons in the dooket the police come over to talk to us.

"Have you seen anyone in the backdoor," they ask.

"No we haven't" I say.

"Some guy was assaulted with a knife," they say.

"No we havenae seen nobody."

CHAPTER 29

"Where are you going today," my mam asks. "Out with Halfpint? Your wee gang of pals are getting bigger."

"I know mam. Lassies are wanting to hang about with us tae."

"Look at you," mam says.

"Am just going to Falcon shops. That's where we meet up."

When we get there some of the outher boys are there. Wee Davy - some boy Halfpint stays next to decides for us that we go up the town. We look at all the clothes shops with all the stylish clothes - Cowans, Jaffa, Saxons. My eyes light up.

Davy says, "Look they take prova cheques."

"Provedent you mean" I say.

Then we go into clothes shop at Orr square.

"Nice clobber here," Davy says.

We go into Boots and up the stairs. They sell LP records. I start to get into a band called Mott the Hoopel. I go and get a carrier bag. "Keep a lookout Davy." I say.

I try tay get the records in the bag. They fit in, so in they go. I head out the shop. The boys come out laffing. We meet the girls. We show them the records. They want to buy them and I sell them.

My god I have went from nicking pick'n'mix out of Woolworths to records. On the way home we decide to get jobs to get clothes that are in style.

When a get home I say to my mam, "Am going to work down the farm me and Franky worked in last summer mam. Will you get me a provedent check if I give you it off my pay on a Friday? We want to be smart mam."

"Ok," she says. She knows I will.

"Am away out wi the boys."

We head down to Minzees for a carry out.

We get one of the older guys that sit up in the Railway Inn - that's the old railway bridge in Inkerman - to get us it. We get a flagen of cider and bottles of Old England wine. We sit on the bridge. Docky and Jake have a pound bet to see who can drink the bottle of wine in one go.

Jake wins again. His legs are hollow.

"We are going up the town now,"Halfpint says.

I say, "Did you tell your mam about getting a job? Am going back down the farm?"

"I've got a job tae," Halfpint says, "As an apprentice welder."

He is a year older than me. We head up the town. We're walking down the street - me and Halfpint. Then we hear a crash coming from in front of us. It comes from the clothes shop in the square. Davey has kicked the in window. Its smashed and he's cut his ankle.

"Whit you doing?" I say to Davey.

"Let's get back to the skeem," Halfpint says.

CHAPTER 30

It's Saturday.

Me and Sandra are going to the shows at the racecourse. We're walking along Feegie Park Avenue and all the women from the scheme are coming back from the shows.

Sandra says, "Look at all the lamps pitchers metal bins and bed sheets, they've won them at the prize bingo Pat."

The Avenue is full of these older women with their wee peenes and open coats, one woman is wearing boots that have fur at the ankle and has a head square.

I shout at Sandra, "You can have a game when we get there, you're the right age!"

Whit a slap I get.

"I'm only kidding," I tell her as I rub my jaw.

You can smell the shows as we walk down Greenhill Road. The smell of onions and the music playing - See My Baby, Jive Wizard, David Bowie, Slade.

We climb the stairs at the motorbikes then we go on the Walzers. I see my favourite hot doughnuts with sugar.

I get a bag and I start to eat.

Then Sandra says, "Can I have one?"

I look in the bag and they're finished.

She laughs, "You were in a daze eating them."

We hear screams and see a big fight. Police and guys are fighting.

I say to Sandra, "Come on let's get out of here I'm no getting caught up in that."

As we head home the black Maria's police van's going in.

"You coming up to mine Sandra?" I ask. "We'll watch a film, Don't Watch Along is on."

"Then I've got to walk hame efter it," Sandra says.

"I'll walk you hame," I tell her. "Not late though as me and Franky have an interview for a job in the rope works **tomorrow**."

Sandra smiles, "That's good that means you'll get a full-time job."

Me and Franky go for the interview. We get the part-time job on the farm. But we tell the farmer we want full-time jobs.

He says, "Well gie the rope work a go Pat if you want mate."

CHAPTER 31

Am waiting on the tractor with the tailor with the rest of the Feegie folk. We are all out for the one thing. To put food in our families mouths. I'm standing there with Sandra my new girlfriend.

"Ooo is that the new girlfriend? A wee winch afore work is it?"

It's big May and Lillian - the women I work with in the totties. The three of us work together. They are as hard as nails. And their tungs, they wood strip paint aff a door!

"Hope she's no burning you out wi aw that smoochin. Need ta get him Johnny bags, Lillian, for the weekend," May shouts.

"I've got some May I'll bring them in."

I'm embarrassed but know they are only joking. I'm staking the sacks of totties onto the tractor. They are filling their big sacks with these totties. Then it happens ma trousers bust underneath. FK!

Trying to hide I bend down to pick a sack up.

May notices my trousers have bust and i have nae pants on. Ma pants are in the wash.

My willie faws out and May bends down and goes, "Tickle tickle. Hey Lillian, it's a small one he needs then!"

The farmer comes over after dinner and asks me to go work somewhere else. Big May lets out a roar.

The farmers a big man about 6 feet 4 but the women don't care.

They ball him out, "Pat's our boy, Fk off."

And he does.

He tells me, "Just keep working wi they two if your ok wee man."

"That's ok way me mister farmer."

We finish up at five. I get the tractor to the keep left. But my worst nightmare has come true. Sandra's waiting on me she has finished her work.

She works in the playtex factory.

"Whit am a going to do May?"

"Whit about?" she asks.

"My trousers are bust and my wullie is falling out."

Lillian gives me her cardigan to wrap around me.

"See you in the morning pal," they shout.

CHAPTER 32

Me and big Sandra are walking alang the Avenue. She says, "Take that cardigan off it's like ma granny's peena wrapped round you."

"I cant," I say.

"How no?"

"Ah've bust my trousers and Ah'v nae pants on."

Sandra grabs the cardigan and laffs.

"Sandra, Sandra gimme that! Ma willie will fall out."

She giggles, "Let me see, come on."

We go to ma house to get changed. We get to ma close. I tell her to wait cause I don't want ma mam to see her. Am in the room changing my trousers and my worst nightmare is coming true.

My big brother Joe, "Well, well mam, he isn't a gentleman. He's left his girlfriend in the cold damp close wi no lights on,"

I come out the room. Ma mam is wi Sandra.

"Whit the fuck are you doing?" I ask her

"Right Pat, that's enough of that language in front of the young lassie," ma mam says.

I rush Sandra out, "Come on Sandra, come on."

"Your mams lovely," Sandra says.

"Ah no, just that Joe embarrassing me," I say.

Sandra laughs, "Don't worry at least your willie will no get cold now."

We meet Franky and May and fancy the Boston cafe on Well Street. We have ice cream drink - cola wi ice cream

"Are your lights still off Pat?" Franky asks.

"Aye ma da's still on the drink."

"I've got an idea," he says.

"Whit?"

"Later."

We walk the girls hame. I go up to Sandra's landing. Franky and May stay at the bottom. We're having a winch when Sandra starts to bite my neck.

"Whit you daeing Sandra?!"

She laffs and says, "Come here."

And we kiss again. She goes for my neck again.

I say, "Did you no have enough to eat in the café?"

We laff.

Me and Franky head home. We pass the chapel.

Franky says, "Come on."

We go to the door. It's open. We go into the chapel. We stand where people put 10p in a box and light a candle to pray for someone. I leave 10p and run out wi the box of candles. I get hame and go in the house.

The lights are still off. There's only half a candle left.

I smile and gie my mam the box of candles.

CHAPTER 33

Sunday. My mam is going to mass. She says to me, "Do you want to come with me?"

I look at her, "No mam."

"How no?" she asks.

"The priest might ask for his candles back and you've used them."

My mam smiles, "I'm making a nice dinner."

"Is ma dad no going to the Green Hill hotel for a drink?"

"Hez gone."

Dinner time comes. My mam has made a lovely dinner. Roast beef and totties. After dinner my mam gives me a bowl and sends me to the ice cream van for a big bowl of ice cream.

CHAPTER 34

It's a misty summer morning. I am up ready to go work on the farm. I go in the kitchen. On the table there is a tea pot wi a tea cosy on it. Ma mam pours me a cup of tea

"Thats the best cup of tea ma."

She says, "It's stewed."

"AAA love it ma. Strong and sweet."

My mam tells me she has made my favourite - plain bread and butter. It's the butter we get from liptons dairy. Ma mam has got a tik book in there for when we run out of money through the week.

We always run out of money.

Mams told me I havnae to break into shops anymore. "Theres chopped pork on they pieces," mam says. "Only the best for ma boys."

"Hey mam give him extra," Joe says. "He might start to come hame late. You know wa another woman in his life." He shouts, "Your chucked mam!"

"Don't listen to him ma," I say.

"Am away to work."

"Your early the day," my mams says.

Joe laffs, "He's in love mam, they kiss at the keep left before he starts work on the totties."

CHAPTER 35

I am up in the bathroom before Joe my big brother.

Before he gets in, he shouts, "Am in first."

But am in already. He always leaves the place stinking, then I have to go in. So im in first today. He's no happy.

Mam shouts. "Stop your fighting boys or I'll hit the two of yous wa the boiler stick!"

I walk into the kitchen. Ma mam is putting out the tea. I've no got dressed yet and I have no tap on.

Then I hear his voice, "Look at his neck mam, a think Dracula sleeped way him," Joe laffs.

Ma mam grabs my head and looks at my neck, "Whit is that?! Does Sandra's maw no feed her? I'm coming wi you to the Keep left when you meet her."

"Whit fur," I say.

"Whit fur? Whit fur? Look at the state of your neck."

"Don't do that mam it wont happen again promise."

Theres a knock at the door.

"There's Franky for you."

We head to get picked up for work and meet Sandra before she goes to work.

When we get there, there's a man with a clip board. He pulls me aside. He tells me he is the school board. Says he was told me and Franky were working on the farm.

The tractor comes.

And the man with the clipboard says, "You're going to school."

Then May and ma pal Lilian and others start on him.

What a mouth full he gets. So he walks away. We go to work and get in the field and work away.

Then its tea break. Me and the two women are having our pieces.

May notices my neck, "Hey come here."

She grabs me and shouts, "Lillian look, a bookie badge."

Lillian laffs and opens a packet, "I've got something for him May."

Then she hands me something. "Here's a jonnie!"

I look at it and say, "That's massive, you must be married to the jolly giant!"

She busts out laffing.

"That's a good answer," May says. "He got you there Lillian."

CHAPTER 36

It's Friday night and a have came hame fa working on the farm. I didn't meet Sandra as I do every night. I am making my way alang Feegie Park Avenue. I have a sicking feeling in my belly. I get to the close. Going up the stairs I can tell somethings rang. I go in the door my brother Joe gets me in the lobbie.

"Don't kid my mam on," he says. "He hasen't come home again with his wages."

I walk in the kitchen. "Hi mam. Here is my dig money and a wee bit extra," I say.

"Thanks son."

I can tell shes crying.

"It's only chips eggs and beans Pat," she says.

I smile. "That's my favourite."

Joe says, "Here is my dig money mam. And a have gave you a bit extra."

The door goes.

Mam goes, "Shhhh."

Its the provedent woman. The debt collector.

My mams face is full o fear. "Kid on were no in," she says. "I've no got it this week."

I get up and go to the door. Am nearly crying.

I say to the woman, "My mam no got it this week am sorry."

The woman says, "Its ok Pat."

I go back in the kitchen.

"What did she say?" Mam asks.

"She said that's ok."

"Were no going back to hiding behind the chairs when the debt collector comes," she says.

"Joe works in a factory, I work on the farm and a plunk school to work. And you do two jobs **Mam**. For him to come in drunk with no fucking wages. It's no happening anymore."

I go away to see Sandra. When I get there she **asks** where I wiz.

"I had to go straight hame. Coming down the shows?"

She said ok.

We can smell the shows before we get to the bottom of the Avenue. We get to the shows we go on the Walzers and the motorbikes. We go a wee walk. I get my mam a wee bag of chips.

When I go in the door joe grabs me. "He is in his bed drunk," he says. "No wages."

"No wages?" I say.

"Fk it," Joe says. "Come on."

"No," Mam says. "I don't want youse to do this."

"Got to mum sorry."

Joe holds the door open the lights are out. I can smell drink from the room. I crawl along the floor like a soldier in my wee war comic I get fa yankeemanks a shop in the west end. I get to ma dads trousers.

Am shiteing myself.

I go through his pockets. Change that's all. And his fag packet. I open his fag packet to steal a few fags.

Inside the fag packet is paper money rolled up like fags.

"Dirty fly basterd," Joe says.

I take the lot and crawl out the room. We go in the living room. My mams sitting wi the piece'n'chips I got her. I give her all the money.

She's got a tear in her eye, "I didn't want that," she says.

"It had to be done mam. We're working hard along with you to keep food on the table not drink in his belly."

My Mam smiles.

"Am away out for a fag," I say.

"Whit?!"

"A mean fresh air."

Ma mam doesn't know I smoke.

"Puffing Billy," she says.

CHAPTER 37

I get ready for my work come Monday. I'm up early, I couldn't sleep.

Franky's late.

I head down to Clark Street and go into the rope works. Nae Franky and am no enjoying this job. But I door it out.

The horn goes and am out of there but ave got a horrible feeling. I head up the road.

I get into the hoose and my mam says, "Sit down son."

I cannae sit down, I no there's something wrong.

"Whits wrong with you mam? Tell me"

She smiles at me, "It's no me."

I cuddle my mam and nearly cry with relief but that's short lived.

"Sit down Pat."

"Why?"

"Just sit down."

I sit down. My mam looks at me.

She breaths in, "Its Franky."

I stop her speakin, "I no he's no going to the rope work. That's ok. That jobs shite. We're going to the farm in the morning."

She bursts out crying.

"Whits fucking up mam? Tell me."

"Franky, Franky is dead."

I cant take it in.

She says it again, "Did you hear me Pat? Franky is dead."

"No, no, no, don't tell me that."

"He went swimming on his camping holiday and got into trouble," she says.

And I run out the house.

CHAPTER 38

The night my mam told me about Franky I run out the house. I just don't know what to do – I have an empty feeling. I come down the stairs from my house. We stay on the top floor. There are flower pots on the window ledges on every winda.

I didna know I hit them off on the way down.

Miss Kyle comes out when she hears the smashing and gives me a row. I tell her to fuck off. Poor woman.

And I run out the close.

Every wall in the close is coming in to meet me I just have to get out. I can't breath.

I get onto Ferguslie Park Avenue. It is so long with big tenements closes on either side with big trees on each side. I have a picture in my mind of me and Franky climbing the trees to look on birds nests. They were so high but we were never feart.

I walk to the top of the Avenue and folk are saying hello. I ignore them.

It is getting late and dark.

I hear a voice, "Pat, Pat come here son."

I cry, "No leave me alone."

A man grabs me and cuddles me.

I didn't hear him cry.

And there we are in the Avenue of the hardest housing skeem in Scotland if not Britain - a man crying along with a young boy.

It is my dad.

The first time I have ever seen my dad cry.

We sit on the kerb and my dad starts to talk to me, "Listen let's me and you be pals."

I look at him, "No. Whit do you care? You don't come home most Friday's. And we struggle. Me. My brother Joe. And my lovely hard fucking working mam for you to get drunk."

"I know," he says and then, "I promise you it won't happen again. I promise you it's hurting me seeing you hurt. It's the first time you've felt hurt."

And I say, "No its no, I feel hurt on a Friday. On a Friday when you dinnae come hame."

And I am crying in the avenue of Ferguslie wi my da and Frank is dead.

CHAPTER 39

One night, after Franky's funeral I say to my mam, "I don't want to go back to that job."

"What you talking about? You have always worked." She says,

And then a voice and it wasn't my mams voice, "Your not stopping working when you live under my roof." My dad.

"Whit are you talking about? My boy has always worked and brought his wages home. Mare that you have done. You were meant to stay aff the drink to help Pat. And youv no." My mam was mad at ma dad.

He was just about to start arguing and I say, "No you haven't stayed aff the f'king drink. You don't care about anybody. All you care about is where you get your next drink fae."

I run out the hoose.

I go up the west end and into shops. I start asking for a job. I get a job in McDowalls the butchers.

Mr McDowell is a lovely man. He sits me down and asks me why I left the rope work. I tell him about Frank dying. And I tell him about my dad's broken promises.

He gives me a cup of tea and says, "Its not easy for your dad to stop drinking just like that. You come here tomorrow at six and start working. We will get on like a house on fire."

I head home. I just want to tell my mam I got a job. She is so happy.

CHAPTER 40

Mr McDowall asks me, "Do you go to the football?"

"I go to Love Street. I get a lifty over with my pals some Saturdays," I say.

"That's good son," he says. Then he says, "Bill, train that boy. He is a good one."

He starts to show me things to do. But when the shop gets busy he serves. I look for things to do. I go in the big kitchen and fill up the sinks. One with soapy water and one with clean water. I wash all the chrome plate and trays and tubs. Am sorting them out in order.

I hear Bill and Mr McDowalls voice, "Where is Pat?"

One of the men says, "In the kitchen."

They open the door.

"My god, well done son. You weren't asked to do that."

"Bill was busy," I say. "I didn't want to sit about doing nothing so I looked for something to do that no one needed to show me."

"Brilliant!" Mr McDowall says.

"Where do the trays and tubs go? I will put them away and clean the sinks."

"Can you make sausage Pat?"

"Aye I can do that."

"Then we will have rolls and sausage. That's a good boy we got there." Mr McDowall says. "Pat the butters in the fridge."

"Where is the fridge?"

Bill takes me into a big room that's got meat hanging in it. I rubs my head and laffs, "That's the fridge!"

I make the rolls and the tea. Then I go through the front shop and go to give the boss my money for my rolls.

"Whits that for Pat?"

"My rolls and sausage Mr McDowall," I say.

"It's ok, the shop takes care of that pal."

I walk away.

He shouts on me, "Pat, thanks son."

"What for boss?" I ask.

"For doing that."

"I just wanted to pay ma way and not take advantage."

After dinner I start to tidy up. I do the same all week. There's an older man. I can tell he doesn't like me.

"What have I done to him?" I ask Bill.

"Nothing wee man. He is just a fly man. Just watch yourself with him."

I clean the back shop.

"Pat can you do me a favour," Bill says.

"Of course, whit you want?"

"Can you do the big bins out the back?"

I pull the two big bins out and put all the bin bags and cardboard in the bins. The bin's full, so I climb in and brake the cardboard boxes up and lay them flat.

I lift a bag out the bin to flatten the cardboard. One of the bags bursts and I notice a long bit of meat in it.

I go in and say to Bill, "Whit do I do with the old meat?"

"Whit old meat?"

"The one in the bag I burst."

Bill comes out. I show him. "That's a full sirloin Pat," he says.

"Whit is that?"

"It's a dear steak."

"I have never had a steak Bill."

The next day Mr McDowall says, "Am making breakfast today. And wee man a steak for you."

"What's that for?"

Bill lafs, "For being you. Have you noticed someone is missing today?"

"Yes that boy that didnae like me."

"Mr McDowall waited in the shop last night till he heard a noise at the bins. Opened the door and the guy that didn't like you was in the bin."

"What wis he doing in the bin?"

"Said he was looking for a bag. Said he'd seen the new boy from Feegie putting some meat in a bag and then in the bin. Said what do you expect o someone from an undesirable area. Wee basterd," Bill says.

"I don't live in the undesirable area."

Mr Mcdowall tells me, "I told him no tae come back tae work. Trying to blame a wee boy that is doing great."

CHAPTER 41

My mam has got me a provedent loan. She has to go up on her dinner break on Tuesday to sign for it. I feel rotten. She is given up her dinner break to go for a loan for me so I can have the same clothes as the boys I hang about with. It's in my head all night.

I go home early.

"Whit you hame for at this time," ma dad says.

"Am working at six in the morning am going to bed," I say.

But there is no fooling my mam. She can tell something is bothering me. She comes in my room with toast and tea.

"Whit is up with you Pat?"

"Nothing," I say.

"I no you too well Pat Kidd and when something bothers you it bothers me. Did you get into bother when you were out?"

"No Mam."

"Whit is it then?"

"I don't want you to go for that loan for me."

She can tell I have a tear in my eye.

"You'll miss your dinner break as well."

"Don't you be daft. You work two jobs so you deserve it."

CHAPTER 42

I am up early. That early the birds are singing. They are doing my head in.

My mam makes me peaces in cheese - plain bread, cheese and real butter. They are wrapped in the paper aff the plane loaf. It keeps them fresh.

I am first at the shop.

Then comes the rest. Mr McDowall has taken me aside. He gives me a butcher overall.

"Can you put the sawdust down Pat," he says

I grab the sawdust and put it all over the floor.

Bill the butcher asks if I can sweep out the chill rooms and put fresh sawdust down.

"I ok pal thanks. Ive finish here."

"Wee man why did you say thanks?" Bill asks.

"Because you asked me to do something. I don't want to stand about doing nothing."

I go into the kitchen. Theres plates and big trays in the big sinks. "Fk I could have a bath in one of them," I say outloud.

So I start to wash the dishes. I get them done. I dry them. Then I say to Bill, "Where do these go pal?"

"Did you wash them?" he asks.

"Yeah. Was I no supposed to?"

"Sorry no Pat you weren't supposed to." He kicks the back door open. "No that lazy bastered oot here was to wash them!"

I tell Bill I don't mind but he shouts to the lads outside,

"Get in there and get the breakfast made and clean up after you."

He asks me what I want for breakfast and I tell him that I have mine. But him and Mr McDowall tell me to take a roll and sausage and have ma peaces at dinner time.

I finish work. I go and meet my mam in the house in Tannahill Terrace.

We are going to be moving there to a new place.

"What do you think Pat," she asks.

"Smashing," I say in a posh voice.

"Do you like it son?"

"I do mam my. And ill have my owen room!"

Ma mams family all muck in to get it dun up. My dad works hard and papers everywhere. My room has wood chip and I put photos of my music comic and St Mirren photos on my wall.

A new hoose and am loving it at the butchers. Am learning to make sausage and links.

On Saturday the boss Mr McDowall – who I call him Jimmy now calls me to him. He asks me how my dad is doing.

"He is trying," I say.

"Are you going to see St Mirren today?" he asks me.

"Yes."

He slips me a fiver.

"Thanks Jimmy!"
Then I meet wee Davy and we go to the game.

CHAPTER 43

My dad works on the garden all weekend. Am proud of him. I go back to work on Monday and the rest of the week. The garden looks great.

My mum is so happy and so am I. But it is short lived.

I leave the butchers on Friday night. I get to the top of king street. I here the sirens of the firebrigade passing me going down to Ferguslie.

I somehow look across to Tannahill. I see the smoke coming out the roof off a house. I head down fast.

Am really afraid.

I get into the street.

Ambulance and firemen coming out ma house with a stretcher.

I am crying but don't let anyone see.

I run into the hoose shouting, "Mam Mam."

A fireman grabs hold of me, "It's not your mum."

Then he says, "It's your dad."

Mam, Joe and Irene tell me he went to bed steaming with a fag and fell asleep.

We go up to hospital. My dad is kept in.

Then he is transferred to another hospital.

He needs to get help with his drink problems. My mam asks me to go with her to see him. "No mam he has had his last fucking chance."

"Please for me," she says.

She can wind me round her finger.

I go with her to the visiting hall. Desks and chairs with folk at them. I sit down with my mam. Joe comes in and sits with us.

My dad comes in. He is crying.

I am nearly crying.

Jo looks across at another table. There are other visitors giving patients cans of beer.

I lose it. I go over. I grab the cans and throw them in the bin.

One of the guys grabs me. I throw him on the ground. Joe and a nurse grab me.

"My dad is in here trying to get aff drink and youre bringing drink in," I say.

CHAPTER 44

When we get my dad home the house has been fixed up. The damage the fire caused my mams famley - Aunt Teresa, Brenda and Merry have been down and done the house up.

My dad comes in. I can see he is crying.

Joe has new job with the parks department doing the gardening in the town.

He becomes the boss.

He comes to my mams one morning with his work mates and drops off slabs for my dad's gardening.

We will be back to lay them.

It is a lovely garden. The boys lay the slabs back and front wie my dad. My mam is so happy. I love to see that.

I am at work and Jimmy (Mr McDowall) the boss asks, "How's your dad?"

"He is doing great Jimmy," I say.

At the end of the day he gives me a parcel of butcher meat.

"I can't afford that," I say.

"You don't need to pay,' he says.

"Your a good boy and your work is great."

I can't wait to go hame. When I get In I say to my dad, "Da come in the kitchen."

I show him whit I have got.

"I hope you haven't stole them. Remember we have changed," he says.

"Mr McDowall gave me them for you."

Ma dad cuts the tripe up and boils it in the house. It is stinking.

"If you bring that hame again I am going to ground you," my mam says.

The garden is looking great. It has flowers all around the borders and the back door planted by my dad. It has his vegetable plots, but Sheba my German Shepherds has peed all over the grass and has burnt the grass.

Ma Dad cuts the burnt bits out.

"Get your shoes on," he says to me and my mam.

We go down to racecourse football park next to the motorway. There is spare bit of grass next to the road. My dad cuts the turf. I put it in his wheelbarrow.

We see a police motor putting his lights on.

Me and my mum start to run.

She shouts, "Run it's the police!"

We get over the road.

His wee wackly leg gets stuck behind the wheelbarrow. He gets caught.

When he gets in he calls us everything.

We can't stop laffing.

CHAPTER 45

My mam and dad win the garden competition. But my mam is away to Ireland with the women to see ideas for the cumunity centre Ferguslie is to get.

My mum is the chairperson of FLAG Ferguslie League of Action Group. They have gone to see how things work in Dublin.

My Mam, her best friend Alice and Frances.

Feegies angel's my dad calls them. My mam says they were in a high flat lift in Dublin.

The lift stopped. The doors opened and a man came in with his horse.

My mam asked him, "Whit you doing with the horse?"

"Taking it up the house."

She looks at him, "That's where we keep wur horses."

My mam never forgot that day.

I ask Frances's years later if it was true.

She says, "Aye Pat, it is."

My mam gets an award from the Head of Scotland and the Queen. My mam and dad then meet the Queen and Prince Philip when she visits Paisley.

My dad gets a cup for his garden. They get their photos taken with them. In the photo you can see Philip laffing at my dad.

"Whit did you say to him," I ask.

"You haven't got a rose named after your wife And I have,' he says to my dad.

And my Dad says, "What's the roses name fur Betty."

The prince laffs.

My dad changed for me. But my mums sisters always likes to come down on a Friday night for a drink. My Dad is welcoming so he is.

He gets a bottle and a half of old England wine. It lasts him all weekend.

I'm proud of you dad.

CHAPTER 46

It's the middle of April. I am sitting alone after losing my mam on the 6th. I am thinking back to what she done to bring us up. The cold frosty mornings. The windows in the house frozen up as she gets us out of bed.

She was always up early to light the fire before we got up, so we were no freezin. She'd drop us at my grans.

Some days she did three jobs and ma old gran would moaning at her because ma dad didnae came hame fa the pub.

I telt ma mam that when I was old enough I would gie her money. Years passed and I didnt go to my secondary school. Thats what a lot of the boys fa Feggie done.

Feegie the preist called it. Ferguslie Park on a Sunday.

But to us it was Feggie.

A wee skeem in Paisley to people that didn't know.

You could smell the farm in the summer nights. The farm we didn't go to school for. Where we picked collies, totties, turnups and got paid daily. I always gave ma mam my wages. She would say no and would have a wee tear in her eye.

"It's for you mam," I'd say, "I love you."

Printed in Great Britain
by Amazon